Beloved Tywi

A Visual Journey

Beloved Tywi

A Visual Journey

KEN DAY

Gomer

Dedicated to Helen, Sam and BB,
who are the light of my life,
and to seekers of that special light.

Published in 2006 by
Gomer Press, Llandysul, Ceredigion, SA44 4JL
www.gomer.co.uk

ISBN 1 84323 651 6

ISBN-13 9781843236511

A CIP record for this title is available from the British Library.

Copyright © photographs: Ken Day, 2006
Copyright © text: the contributors, 2006

Printed and bound in Wales at
Gomer Press, Llandysul, Ceredigion

Contents

Deep Snow in Dinefwr Park.

Foreword

I can't claim, alas, that I hail from this lovely valley, but I'm privileged to live here, and from my window can watch the Tywi flowing towards Llansteffan beneath the bridges of Carmarthen town. But to glimpse the river at its best, I like to walk up Llangynnwr hill and to a bench under a yew tree in the church graveyard. From there you can see as far as Bethlehem and the Black Mountain of the Beacons. Look hard and you can see as far back as the age of Arthur and Merlin and the monasteries; you can almost see Arglwydd Rhys in Dinefwr and Owain Glyndŵr in Dryslwyn; William Salesbury at his desk in Abergwili, translating the New Testament into Welsh and sad Rhiwallon watching the maid disappear back into Llyn y Fan Fach. From here you can see why this county has been called the Garden of Wales.

Enjoy the journey from your armchair … but may this book invite you to the banks of Afon Tywi to see for yourself the water and the wonder.

Ni allaf hawlio fy mod yn tarddu o Ddyffryn Tywi, ond rwyf wedi cael y fraint o ymgartrefu yma, a does dim dwywaith nad yw'r afon yn destun rhyfeddod. O ffenestri'r tŷ, gallwch ei gweld yn llifo o dan bontydd Caerfyrddin. Ond er mwyn ei gweld yn ei holl ogoniant, mae'n well gen i ddringo i eglwys Llangynnwr. Ar fainc ym mynwent yr eglwys honno, gallwch weld ymhell – mor bell â Bethlehem a'r Bannau Bach a Bryniau Caersalem David Charles hyd yn oed. Craffwch a gallwch weld mor bell yn ôl ag amser Arthur a Myrddin a'r mynachlogydd; mor bell â'r Arglwydd Rhys ac Owain Glyndŵr, hanes Abergwili a chyfieithu'r Testament Newydd, a hanes trist Rhiwallon a merch Llyn y Fan Fach. A gallwch weld beth oedd yr ias a deimlodd Gwenallt a pham mai hon yw'r Sir sy'n hawlio'r enw 'Gardd Cymru'. Mwynhewch y lluniau a'r bob cyfri … ond os cewch ryw awr o hamdden, dewch draw am daith a wnaiff eich cyfareddu.

MERERID HOPWOOD

Dinefwr Castle from Cilsan bridge.

Introduction

A week after we first moved to Wales, we visited Llandeilo on a free day and sat overlooking the valley having lunch. In shafts of sunlight, a red kite flew downstream, gliding slowly, and we could look down on the colours of the wings. It was my first sighting and that combination of landscape and bird started the love affair which would culminate in this book.

Later, I had a job that involved travelling the roads of west Wales. I got to know almost every mile of the thousands and every bridge where every new vista deepened my awe at this land. Then I met people living here, people whose families have lived here forever, whose lives, language and culture are embedded here. For others, incomers like me, the Tywi is a constantly unfolding pleasure, new every day. The two kinds of devotion to this landscape – the deep abiding certainty of history, and the awed, look-at-that newness – joined together and the title of the book came into my mind.

The Tywi is nearly 70 miles long and, though I now know it quite well, this book cannot do justice to it. The photographs though are the best I could do to picture the spirit of the river. A book this length, with this many images, could be made from every mile. For more than four years, I had a list of views with angles of light and best time-of-day scrolling constantly past my eyes, ready to go out and make the picture. Most of the images in this book were planned; some though are happy accidents. Being there with a camera when that special view with that special light comes into sight is a rare combination, a joy when it happens, but by nature unreliable. I could never hope to cover every aspect, and I'm certain there are endless possibilities for more photos. My objective has been to give a celebration of the Tywi, a taster of what it is like at its most beautiful. Through the written contributions of over twenty of the valley's inhabitants, I have also tried to capture a sense of what it is like to live here.

KEN DAY

Wales and the Four Sections of the River Tywi

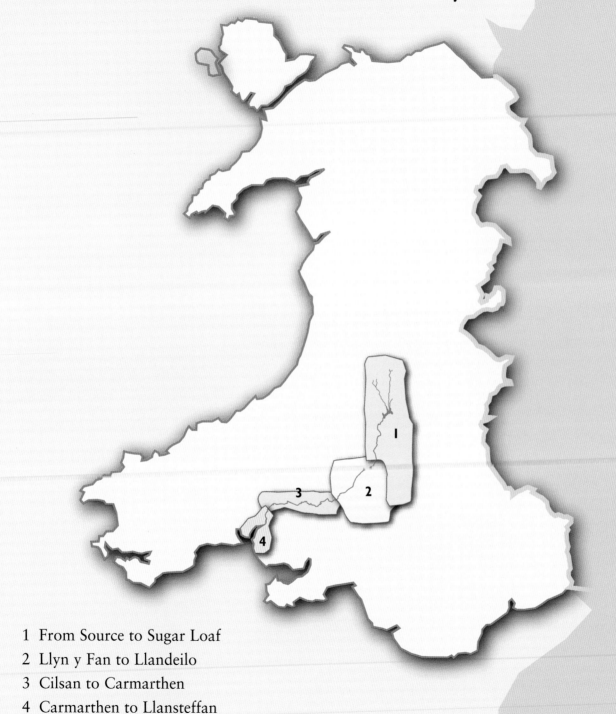

1 From Source to Sugar Loaf
2 Llyn y Fan to Llandeilo
3 Cilsan to Carmarthen
4 Carmarthen to Llansteffan

Section 1

From Source
to Sugar Loaf

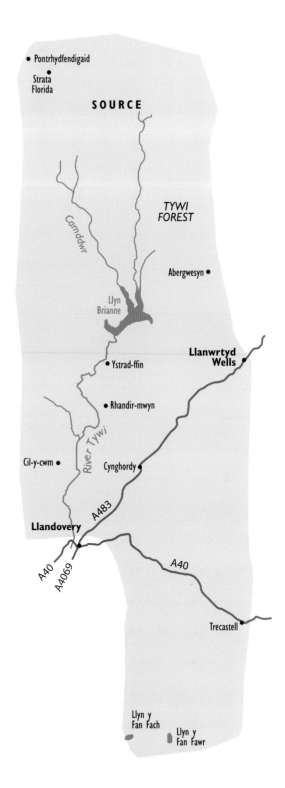

Source of the river Tywi.

(opposite) Looking to the source from the first bridge.

No. 1   Sighting the Source

The Tywi Forest is a wild and remote part of Wales, and visiting the vast uninhabited tract of the Cambrian Mountains gives me the same feeling I had when riding and camping in the Rocky Mountains in America. There are very few unnatural sounds, no houses or tarmac roads, and the wind is fresh and clean. Even though man has altered the landscape – large areas of the mountains have been planted with conifers – it still feels as though it is the same as it has always been, primordial and natural. The Tywi rises in an inaccessible bog just to the north of the Tywi Forest and runs almost due south to Llyn Brianne reservoir. In the river valley and throughout the forest, wildlife is abundant, especially birds of prey such as merlins, red kite and goshawks, and, in the many open wet areas, wading birds can be seen, especially redshanks, curlew, golden plovers and greenshanks. The Forestry Commission is working hard to improve the waterside and other habitats. Opening the tree canopy near the watercourses and varying the ages of the conifer plantations are two ways that are designed to widen the biodiversity and increase populations of birds and mammals.

All Forestry Commission land is open to the public and some areas have ancient rights of way. This is true of the Tywi Forest, which has several very old drover-roads going through it. From Llyn Brianne going north there is an entrance to the forest just before the last road bridge over the river. The gate on the right hand side of the road just before the bridge about four kilometres from the reservoir, is at grid reference 805568, and may need to be opened. It leads to a byway for all traffic alongside the young Tywi for about three kilometres, when, at Moel Prysgau, it reduces in size and heads off to the north-west towards Strata Florida. About one kilometre before this point, though, and to follow the Tywi, you will need to turn right into the forest and follow the cycle way. This is a 'Lôn Las Cymru', a long-distance path, which winds its way up and through the woods for about six kilometres until it comes to the very final crossing of the river. This gravel road is in a working forest, and great care should be taken. Extraction equipment and timber trucks are at work, and the road may be closed occasionally for public safety reasons. The trouble is always worth it, though. The source of the Tywi can be seen about a kilometre to the north from the concrete bridge and is a very special place that very few people know about, let alone visit.

DAVID REES

The river from the forest.

The ford below the first road bridge.

No. 2   The Secret Squirrel

The imposing forests above the upper Tywi valley hold a well-kept secret. Here one of our most appealing native mammals is hidden from all but the lucky few who have glimpsed it amongst the lofty coniferous trees where it spends its life. You could say there is treasure in our forests. But do you have to see this rufous jewel to really appreciate its value to the valley? Now that we can see the world from our living rooms, are our expectations raised too high of what we should see when we are out in the countryside?

For the past three years as biodiversity officer in Carmarthenshire, I have been a part of a project to find out more about the enigmatic red squirrels in the mid-Wales forests, based largely in the upper Tywi valley. During this time I've learnt a lot about this wonderful but elusive creature, which is hanging on for dear life in the woodland above Llyn Brianne reservoir. I've spent time in the forests and seen their feeding signs, I've seen the survey data, and I've even seen photographic evidence. I now know that our red squirrels, once so common but now dramatically declined due to habitat loss and competition and disease from the non-native grey squirrel, do actually exist. Indeed they could help to conserve red squirrels in Wales as a whole. But have I seen one? Not yet. Does it matter? No not really. For me it's enough to know that they are there and that when I go walking through these forests I am lucky enough to be sharing it with such hidden treasure. What we have to consider is the cost of losing them – the forests will be, for so many reasons, a poorer place.

ISABEL MACHO

Waterfall on the Camddwr.

Soar-y-mynydd Chapel.

Llyn Brianne.

No. 3   Living Language

The Welsh language is alive and well in Dyffryn Tywi ('the Tywi valley'), and can be heard in communities throughout the valley. Although the area has seen a decline in the number of Welsh speakers in recent decades, it is encouraging that there has been a big increase in the number of children and young people that can speak Welsh, with the percentage of 3-18 year-olds rising in excess of 80% in many communities across the valley, according to the 2001 census. Dyffryn Tywi is traditionally one of the language's heartlands, with so much of the area's distinctive tradition, heritage, legends and culture inextricably linked with the speaking and writing of Welsh.

I moved from a nearby industrial village to the Llandeilo area in my early teens and therefore spent most of my youth in this lovely rural valley. And I have been fortunate enough to return to live and work in the area. The Welsh language has always played an important part in my upbringing, being the mother tongue of all the family, guiding my way of life through the chapel, schools, my interests and pastimes, as well as other organisations in which I participated.

It is very encouraging today to see the increase in the number of young people embracing the Welsh language and to observe the excitement and new lease of life that this is generating within the communities of the valley through organisations such as Urdd Gobaith Cymru, the Young Farmers' Movement and Menter Bro Dinefwr (the local language initiative and community development agency). Together with other organisations and bodies such as Mudiad Ysgolion Meithrin, Merched y Wawr, local schools and chapels, to name but a few, there are plenty of activities and events through the medium of Welsh for people of all ages and linguistic backgrounds to enjoy.

Such vibrancy, allied with the general goodwill now seen towards the Welsh language, suggests a prosperous future for one of the Tywi's richest resources. Or as the National Anthem puts it: '*O bydded i'r hen iaith barhau*'!

OWAIN SIÔN GRUFFYDD

The Tywi tumbling past Dinas in autumn.

Capel St Paulinus at Ystrad-ffin.

No. 4   RSPB Dinas

The reserve at Dinas, halfway between Rhandir-mwyn and the Llyn Brianne reservoir is a small mountain standing by itself, clad in oak trees. Special for at least 40 breeding species of bird, it is a habitat type known as western upland oak woodland. All the birds at Dinas are typical of that kind of habitat, and the management of the reserve by the RSPB is responsible for ensuring the continuing success of significant numbers of resident as well as migratory species. 250 nest boxes are in place, especially for the pied flycatchers, which in 2006 numbered 97 breeding pairs. On the 60 hectares of Dinas itself, in the same year, other birds include the rarely seen lesser-spotted woodpecker (4 pairs), 65 pairs of redstarts, tree pipits (26 Pairs), 11 great spotted woodpecker couples and 45 pairs of wood warblers. On the Tywi itself, which runs on two sides of Dinas, dippers can be seen as well as common sandpipers, goosanders and grey wagtails. Otters have occasionally been sighted, though I have not had the pleasure of seeing them myself. Of the bigger birds, ravens are a common sight, utilising the many rock faces for nesting, and buzzards regularly patrol the area. The greatest sight, though, and one which never fails to thrill, is of course the red kite. Brought back from the very edge of extinction only recently by very intense conservation measures, there are now an estimated 10-15 pairs nesting within a few square miles.

A little-known fact about the reserve is that it covers a much larger area than Dinas itself. The total area of the Gwenffrwd-Dinas reserve is actually about 690 hectares and includes several farms. The other connected section is to the west and south-west around the Gwenffrwd valley and has a wide diversity of habitat type, ranging from alder woodland in the valley bottoms, through improved grassland to rough upland grazing and heath land on the higher ground. The tenant farmers are encouraged to implement sympathetic management regimes and to be part of the Tir Gofal Welsh Assembly Government supported land management scheme.

MARTIN HUMPHREYS

The youthful Tywi flowing past Dinas.

Tywi Valley from the lead mine in autumn.

No. 5   A Sculpture of Sacrifice

On September 16th, 1400, Owain Glyndŵr began a sixteen-year-long struggle to gain Welsh independence. He roundly defeated Henry IV's army at Hyddgen on the slopes of Pumlumon in the summer of 1401 and then marched victoriously into southern Wales. In response Henry led a huge army from Worcester to capture Glyndŵr and crush the rising in its early stages. He arrived in the Llandovery area and press-ganged Llywelyn ap Gruffydd Fychan, a landowner from Caeo who was in his mid 60s, into his service to help him find Glyndŵr's base.

Llywelyn was known as a host of great generosity and was well loved by his people. He had two sons serving in Glyndŵr's army and determined never to betray his country, family or prince. He led the English king through the uplands of Deheubarth for several wasted weeks on a wild goose chase to allow Glyndŵr the chance to make his escape to Gwynedd where he could consolidate a position of strength.

Henry eventually lost his patience and Llywelyn was forced to admit that he was a loyal follower of Glyndŵr and believed passionately in the cause of Welsh freedom. From the outset he knew what fate lay in store for him but was prepared to make the ultimate sacrifice so that others could carry on the struggle. Henry had Llywelyn dragged to Llandovery where, at the gallows in front of the castle gates, he was publicly disembowelled and dismembered. The torture lasted for hours before death released him from his agony. His salted remains were sent to other Welsh towns for exhibition in order to deter patriots from joining Glyndŵr's army, but ironically this barbaric act had quite the opposite effect.

In the face of impossible military odds, Glyndŵr's war of liberation eventually faltered. But he was never captured or betrayed and had united the whole nation behind his cause. Of Llywelyn, who tenaciously refused to betray his people or accept the bribes and privileges dispensed by a tyrant, we can truly say, 'there was no braver heart'.

In the summer of 1998, local societies, groups and individuals decided that one of Llandovery's greatest heroes should have a fitting monument to honour his memory and the cause he died for 600 years ago. A Memorial Committee was formed which soon gathered support from all sections of the community. An exhibition of the five short-listed submissions was held during the spring of 2000 and the public were asked to express their preferences. The winning design was that created by the brothers Toby and Gideon Petersen of St Clears.

Their 16ft stainless-steel sculpture stands on a 17-tonne stone brought from the hills to the north of the town. It is a memorial that encapsulates the spirit that has sustained the Welsh nation to this day and which has enabled the Welsh people, their culture and language to survive despite the many threats to their existence over the last two millennia. What is more, it celebrates the universal virtues of courage and loyalty.

Over two thousand people attended the unveiling ceremony on October 6th 2001. The magnificent statue has already become associated with Blaenau Tywi, not just as a symbol of its past but also a beacon for its future.

RHOBERT AP STEFFAN

27

Llandovery and Llywelyn ap Gruffudd Fychan's sculpture.

Llandovery town centre.

No. 6   The Heart of Wales

One of Britain's most beautiful train journeys, the Heart of Wales line starts in Swansea and runs, single track for most of the way, to Shrewsbury. On its journey it passes through a significant part of the Tywi valley. As the line comes up from Llanelli and about halfway between Ammanford and Llandeilo, it runs along side the Cennen River, a tributary that joins the Tywi at Ffairfach. From here it follows the valley bottom to Llandovery, and on the way provides stunning views of the meandering river and the hills and ancient hill forts on each side. At Llandovery itself, the line veers northwest towards Llanwrtyd Wells following the valley of another tributary, the Brân. Before it reaches the headwaters at the Sugar Loaf, it passes over the spectacular Victorian viaduct at Cynghordy. Stone built, this 18-arched feat of engineering is 93 feet high and over 650 feet long.

KEN DAY

Cynghordy train viaduct.

William Williams (1717-1791)

Williams Pantycelyn is one of the undoubted greats of Welsh literature. He was the author of poems, numerous and various important prose works and was one of the most famous and influential preachers of his day. But it is for his hymns that he is most famous – and for reasons that will become abundantly clear. He wrote nearly 1,000 hymns and many of those are as famous today as they were during Pantycelyn's own lifetime, when his words defined the spirit of the Great Revival that spread across the length and breadth of Wales in the second half of the eighteenth century.

Many commentators have stated that Pantycelyn is the greatest of all Welsh poets. Others have called him the 'incomparable folk poet of the Welsh' – and it is certain that these people have a very strong case for using such enthusiastic praise!

Williams's Memorial in Llanfair-ar-y-bryn.

It is no exaggeration to say that much of the 'Welsh character' that we recognise today – and which is recognised outside Wales – derives in no small part from the life and works of Williams Pantycelyn. His hymns live on in the language of Wales (both in Welsh and English), and in Welsh ideas about religion and life. It might even be said that Pantycelyn and his hymns provided us with the familiar image of the impassioned, fiery, religious Welshman.

And even if the religious circumstances of Pantycelyn's times – the bubbling cauldron of Methodism, the highly contagious revival spirit and the physical feeling of knowing God – are largely unfamiliar to us today, the hymns still assert their power when they are read and, crucially, when they are sung.

Guide me, O thou great Jehovah,
    pilgrim through this barren land;
I am weak, but thou art mighty,
    hold me with thy powerful hand:
bread of heaven! bread of heaven!
feed me now and evermore.

Open now the crystal fountain
    whence the healing stream doth flow;
let the fiery, cloudy pillar
    lead me all my journey through:
strong deliverer, strong deliverer,
be thou still my strength and shield.

When I tread the verge of Jordan,
    bid my anxious fears subside:
death of death, and hell's destruction,
    land me safe on Canaan's side:
songs of praises, songs of praises
I will ever give to thee.

From *William Williams* by Iestyn Roberts (*Cip ar Gymru/Wonder of Wales* Series)

River Gwydderig at Pont Melin-Guto.

View south from Sugar Loaf.

The Bannau from Llanddeusant.

Llyn y Fan to Llandeilo

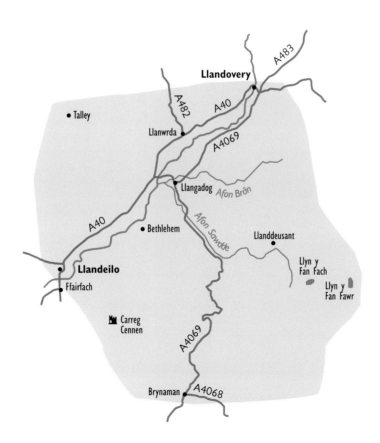

No. 8 The Physicians of Myddfai

The origins of this family of country doctors, whose healing abilities were themselves legendary, popularly derive from a folk tale about Llyn y Fan Fach. Here are examples of their prescriptions.

'A cold mouth and warm feet will live long.

Good are a salmon and a sermon in Lent.

Suppers kill more than the Physicians of Myddfai can cure.

A light dinner and less supper, sound sleep, and a long life.

If thou desirest to die, eat cabbage in August.

To oblige a Man to confess what He has done wrong

Take a frog alive from the water. Extract its tongue and put him back again in the water. Lay the same tongue on the heart of the sleeping man, and he will confess his deeds in his sleep.

A way in which things can be seen which are invisible to others

Take the gall of a cat and hen's fat, mixing them together. Put this in your eyes, and you will see things which are invisible to others.

To extract a Tooth without Pain

Take some newts, by some called lizard, and those nasty beetles which are found in ferns during summer, calcine them in an iron pot, and make a powder thereof. Wet the forefinger of the right hand, insert it in the powder, and apply it to the tooth frequently, refraining from spitting it off, when the tooth will fall away without pain. It is proven.'

from *Folk Tales of Wales* by Eirwen Jones.

Picws Du and Llyn y Fan.

Carreg Cennen Castle in the rain.

Satisfying the Spirit

The breathtaking scenery of the Tywi valley in Carmarthenshire, filling the visual senses from so many different angles, is further enhanced by the sight of so many ancient churches which have stood sentinel over their parishes and peoples for – in many cases – well over 1,400 years.

There are not many Rural Deaneries in the British Isles that can boast such a concentration of ancient sites of worship, all within 212,000 acres. The 'Llan-' prefix of so many of the valley's villages refers to the *Llan*, or circular enclosure that contains 'God's Acre', and gives a clue to the antiquity of the sites. In the east is the 'Llan' of the Two Saints (Llanddeusant), a Romano-Christian site deep in the fastness of a hidden valley, brooded over by the escarpment of the Carmarthen Van (Bannau Sir Gâr) with its wheeling red kites. From here we can head for

Llangadog church.

Llandeilo and its church dedicated to the tutor of St David, then along a valley dotted with estate church gems such as Cwrt Henri, St Paul's, Maesteilo and Holy Trinity, Pontargothi. After reaching the remote Talley Abbey and its neighbour church of St Michael, we can venture to the western Cambrian Mountains and the churches of Caeo and Llansawel. So many fascinating buildings to visit and histories to assimilate that, in this beautiful area, we are set about by an embarrassment of riches for the walker, historian, naturalist, genealogist, day-tripper and spirituality-seeker alike. The trail follower with a car will come across many historic delights along the flat lands of the valley bottom, from the impressive church of St Cadog in Llangadog and St Cathen's, Llangathen, hard by Aberglasney House, to the remote settlements of Llanfihangel Rhos-y-corn in the Brechfa forest and St Paulinus, Ystrad-ffin, with its connections to the great abbey at Strata Florida; all diverse and fascinating living testimonies to the Age of Saints.

Not just, however, for the senses and historic curiosity of the passer-by and resident alike are these varied parishes so important. In these churches, so often remote and hidden, are living and worshipping communities, conforming to the ancient rhythms of observance, still tenacious and determined in their relationships with Christ, yet open to the challenges of today and forging new commitment to take them into the 21st Century. The two towns of Llandovery and Llandeilo, together with all the other 28 village parishes in the Deanery, are moving forward together in an initiative of the Diocese of St Davids to 'Venture in Mission', *Mentro mewn Cenhadaeth*. Through this, the intention is to reinvigorate the worship and increase the relevance of the church's impact in today's world, feeding from well springs of the ancient resources that originate in the life and legacy of so many Celtic saints. For those who have a half-day, a day, a week or a lifetime, the unique churches of the Tywi valley will provide deep satisfaction for the mind, body and spirit.

MIKE COTTAM

(opposite) Sawdde gorge.

The Tywi from Llangadog bridge.

Standing stone near Llangadog.

Garn Goch

The great Iron Age hill fort of Garn Goch dominates the central Tywi valley between Llandeilo and Llangadog. It is in fact two hill forts not one. The larger of the two forts (Gaer Fawr) occupies the eastern summit of the hill and is one of the largest in Wales. A single, massive, collapsed stone wall surrounds an area of eleven hectares. The western section is truly monumental and rises to 6.5m high and some 25m wide. The main entrances were probably on the western and eastern sides although several smaller gaps in the rampart can be seen on the north and south sides. There are traces of at least one roundhouse platform within the interior as well as a large oval cairn, which may be an earlier Neolithic or Bronze Age burial mound. The smaller fort (Gaer Fach) occupies a circular hill summit to the west of the main fort.

One can only imagine the impact that such a massive structure would have had on the surrounding farming community. Clearly, the Celtic chief responsible for its construction would have held significant power over a very large area. Today the bracken that covers the hill fort turns a rusty-red colour in the autumn, making the site stand out against the surrounding green fields and making its name highly appropriate.

GWILYM HUGHES

Meanders near Bethlehem.

44

Llandeilo in the snow.

Pink Mist, Blue Dawn.

No. 11   Fortresses and Farmsteads

The rich farmlands of the Tywi contain many hill forts, from huge fortresses to small defended farmsteads, constructed and in use from the late Bronze Age, through the Iron Age and into the Roman period. Some sites have no surviving earthworks, the only clues to their existence being their dramatic locations and place names preserved in the ancient Welsh language, such as Dinas Bach and Dinas Fawr in Rhandir-mwyn, Mandinam, Llangadog and Castell Gwrychion, Llangathen. Others are indicated by discrete grassy mounds or tumbled stone walls. All were built with defence in mind, and the choice of steep-sided hilltops with impressive views can still have a dramatic effect and saved many from destruction by later development. Though Garn Goch is the best example (and easiest to visit), below it is Llwyndu Camp and northwards are Maes Castell and Bryngwyn, both small but with impressive earth banks and in stunning locations, while to the west is the wooded hill of Carreg Cegyn with its large west-facing rampart. Further west, past Llandeilo is Grongaer hill, with large earth banks still intact and Bryn Myrddin, also later used as a Roman camp. Looking down from these ancient sites it is just possible to imagine the landscape as it would have been; many of the field boundaries, lanes and paths date from these early times when the land was first divided up. In fact the local rural population at this time was much greater than it is now, with largely self-sufficient communities linked to the wider world through trade, in which the Tywi played an important part.

JASON LAWDAY

46

No. 12   Ghosts of the Golden Age

I was first introduced to Dinefwr in 1990 when I started working for the National Trust in Llandeilo. Initially, I was aware of this 'place' on the outskirts of Llandeilo that was exciting my colleagues and which had been the subject of a recent successful public appeal. Why was this relatively unknown place deemed important enough to justify all this attention and money?

The National Eisteddfod came to Llandeilo in 1996 and some competitive poetry singing the praises of Dinefwr and the 'golden age' of Wales was brought to my attention – the light was turned on! This was a place that lies deep in the national consciousness of Wales. I began to discover the emotion that the place engenders and to appreciate that Dinefwr was so much more than a very beautiful place.

Around the old castle the ghosts of the great medieval Welsh kings and princes of the ancient kingdoms of Dyfed and Deheubarth – Rhodri Mawr, Hywel Dda, Rhys ap Tewdwr, Arglwydd ('the Lord') Rhys – inhabit Dinefwr. The role they played in nation building makes this a most enigmatic place. As I understood more, I started to relate the stories of Dinefwr to others, describing not only the roles played by key figures in its history but also the 700-year-old oak trees, along with the noble lineage of the White Park cattle which goes back more than a thousand years at Dinefwr and now roam the ancient Deer Park.

This journey goes on with the 'discovery' of an Iron Age fort in the park whilst, under the ground, two impressive Roman Forts have been identified. This legacy is the result of the 600-year continuity of ownership by the Rhys, later Rice, family, leaving us one of the most beautifully designed landscape parks to be found anywhere in Britain.

PHILIP JAMES

White Park cattle and Dinefwr Castle.

Newton House, Dinefwr Park, Llandeilo.

Ancient oaks in Dinefwr Park.

No. 13   Farming High and Low

As the mists rise over Ystrad Tywi, take the narrow, winding lanes up to the mountains, the islands in the mist where the tributaries that feed the river Tywi have their source in spring-fed streams. Change there has been, but continuity too; this upland landscape with its wide horizons records the deep history of links through time and place with the valley below. Walk in the forests and see the standing stones and burial mounds of the first farmers, the early settlers who followed the rivers to reclaim the land after the glaciers had melted. Curving earth banks and sunken tracks remain to mark the areas of their activity, their settlements and agricultural endeavours.

Come forward in time and discover traces of the summer dwellings and dairies of the people who brought their cattle up from winter housing in the valley farmsteads; follow the tracks of the drovers, funnelling down from summer pasturage to start the long journey to the meat markets of industrial England. Turn a corner and find the straight, wide roads and regular field systems of upland enclosure, driven by economic contingency and the need for increased agricultural productivity to feed the home market. Here are the long, low farmhouses with cattle byres attached, and outbuildings with stables to house the horses that once pulled the plough.

Today the wide horizons remain above this patchwork landscape, looking down over Ystrad Tywi. Although the decline in the dairy industry is reflected in the recent closure of the last creamery in the valley, the swing in emphasis of agricultural schemes from headage to environmental sustainability has enabled continuity through change. Newly replanted hedgerows grow on old earth banks and summer pastures are splashed with the colour of wild flowers, while redundant outbuildings are converted into visitor accommodation and specialist workshops. Listen to the song of the skylarks, their nesting sites now protected, and reflect on the age-old links between these Tywi uplands and the valley below.

PAM STEANE PRICE

49

Dinefwr sunset.

Morning mist from Llandeilo bridge.

Cilsan to Carmarthen

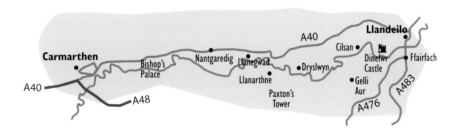

Dinefwr from Cilsan Bridge.

No. 14   A Sudden Flash of Silver

They say the Tywi is the best sea-trout river in Europe. There is no doubting it certainly was, that is, until recently. Maybe the sewin (for so are they locally called) will one day return again in such numbers as I remember in the summers of fifty years ago when you could view from any bridge the river bed 'paved with fish', and at evening the surface of the water everywhere ringed with the splashes of rising fish. It was a sight to behold, and people travelled miles to see the spectacle.

Scarcity of sufficient natural food in the upper reaches of rivers such as the Tywi to bring them into breeding condition causes some of the resident brown trout to turn silver and migrate to sea: strangely, mainly the females. When as adult fish they return on migration to spawn you may, by observation, appreciate why they are known as sewin. Look over Nantgaredig bridge on a sunny day in late spring or summer. It's best to be wearing polaroid glasses. When your eyes become accustomed, among the parallel shadows you assumed were weeds, a sudden flash of silver will glare from one of them in the depths of the swirly upstream pool – a sewin, 'silver one', asserting her space. Fifty at a time will shoal there. Time was when it would have been five hundred or a thousand.

There are salmon to be seen too, occasionally. They do not flash their sides, but you need expertise to tell the difference between them and the big sewin. Some weighing above ten pounds run the Tywi early on. The biggest ever caught on rod and line is said to have been 19½ lbs, date in 1932, place and captor long forgot. The coracles at Carmarthen at one time used to catch sewin of twenty pounds and more. William Elias recorded one of 22lbs.

Look upstream from Nantgaredig bridge, towards some unwisely planted poplars on the left bank beyond the ripple signifying Mari Pool, and that's where, in 1927, the biggest rod-caught salmon was snared. It was a fifty pounder. And it was grassed by Dr Alexander Lindsay at what then was named, is now (and forever shall be), Record Pool.

LYNN HUGHES

Dinefwr from Gelli Aur.

Aberglasney. (© Graham Rankin)

Aberglasney Gardens

Aberglasney must be one of the country's most remarkable garden restoration projects. The once grand mansion nestling below Grongaer Hill was so ruined it was generally considered beyond repair and faced a certain and inglorious destiny.

Thanks to the foresight and commitment of local artist and visionary William Wilkins, the fate of Aberglasney was changed. In 1995, the Aberglasney Restoration Trust was formed to try to save from inevitable collapse the unusual garden structures, and what remained of the derelict mansion. With generous financial assistance from Frank Cabot, an American benefactor, restoration commenced in 1998.

In July 1999, the garden opened and the visiting public could see the house and garden being painstakingly transformed in front of their eyes. The restoration process was also portrayed to a nationwide audience by a BBC series that followed the development. It was only after an extensive archaeological investigation that the importance of the garden structures was realised, the Cloister Range and Parapet Walk, once a common feature in early 17th-century gardens, is now thought to be the only example of its kind in the country.

The early history of Aberglasney is not very well documented. Around 1470 Lewis Glyn Cothi, a professional itinerant poet, made what appears to be the first written reference to the site. It praised the owner Rhydderch Ap Rhys for the cultivation of the vines and oaks that grew around the nine green gardens of Aberglasney. Rhydderch's grandson, Sir William Thomas (who was knighted by King Henry VIII), sold Aberglasney to Bishop Rudd of St David's around 1600 and it is he who was credited with rebuilding much of the house and garden.

The best-known occupant of Aberglasney, however, was the poet John Dyer, who lived here during the early 18th century. His most celebrated poems 'The Country Walk' and 'Grongar Hill' describe the beautiful surrounding countryside.

The garden at Aberglasney has been transformed into a plantsman's paradise and is open to visitors every day. Many of the plants it contains are rarely seen in other gardens in the UK and it has recently been described as 'The Bodnant of South Wales'. The garden continues to develop; a recent addition is the 'Ninfarium', a unique sub-tropical garden, created within the ruined central rooms of the mansion.

GRAHAM RANKIN

(© Graham Rankin)

Dryslwyn Castle and valley.

No. 16   A World of Wildlife

The youthful Tywi and its sister tributaries, the Pysgotwr, Doethie and others flow and tumble through the rocky uplands, home to Twm Siôn Cati (an erstwhile Welsh Robin Hood) and the once almost extinct red kite, both fugitives in their time. It is one of Wales's larger rivers, of great beauty and immense ecological significance.

After leaving the uplands with their open sessile oak woods, mossy and fern-rich and full of summertime red flycatchers and redstarts, the broad valley or 'dyffryn' of the Tywi is reached at Llandovery, where the waters of the Brân reinforce its flow.

Below Llandovery, the Tywi valley has a lowland English feel, both in terms of the landscape of prosperous farms and large estates, with flat, flood plain vistas and mature timbered hedgerows and copses, and also the wildlife. Not here will you find the dippers and grey wagtails of the hill rivers but kingfishers, sand martins and – nesting on the shingle shoals – the engaging little ringed plover which here has its Welsh headquarters with about 50 pairs. It only started nesting on the Tywi in 1986, at which time the rare five-spot ladybird was also discovered at Llanwrda; this ladybird was thought to be extinct in Britain, having last been seen at Speyside many years previous.

Otters too have a stronghold on the river and lucky observers (but not me!) have even seen them from Llandeilo or other bridges. Below water there are thriving populations of salmon, lamprey, and bullhead, as well as the enigmatic and little-known allis and twaite shad. Important heronries occur in valley-side woodlands, and the estates at Gelli Aur and Dinefwr hold majestic, venerable trees, of immense value for rare insects and lichens.

At Ferryside-Llansteffan, the great river flows into Carmarthen Bay, to the accompaniment of wintering waders and wildfowl or more exotic birds such as avocet or that increasingly numerous all-white heron, the little egret. Every autumn, sewin (or 'twps y dail') make their pilgrimage upstream to spawn unless, of course, they are caught by fisherman, heron or otter!

IAN MORGAN

Meanders near Dryslwyn.

Dryslwyn Castle and the morning mist.

The river Cothi in autumn.

No. 17   Culture and Creativity

From an arts perspective, the Tywi valley is vibrant with creativity. Its landscape, of course, provides immense inspiration for visual artists and photographers, but dig beneath the obvious and you will find musicians, sculptors, writers, film-makers and many more like-minded souls firmly embedded in the valley.

The area boasts two renowned gardens, namely Aberglasney and the National Botanical Garden of Wales at Llanarthne, which, together with Newton House at Dinefwr, now routinely provide magical back-drops for the performing arts in the area. Numerous festivals pepper the calendar, some steeped in history such as the the Carmarthen Merlin Festival and the Llandeilo Community Festival, which uses different historical and mythical stories each year as an inspiration, whilst others have a more contemporary slant. Several towns and villages have their own annual festival, including Llandovery, Carmarthen and Llansteffan at the mouth of the river. The Llandeilo Festival of Music and Flowers in July attracts classical musicians from all over the world to the valley every year. Another international dimension is provided by the Small Nations Festival in Cil-y-cwm in the upper Tywi, which attracts music of many kinds from many countries.

Welsh language events are numerous, as you would expect where Welsh is spoken in at least half of all households. Choirs, groups, and individuals, adults and children alike, participate with conspicuous success in the annual National Eisteddfod, and many communities still boast their own eisteddfodau. Other events include Gŵyl Dinefwr and Miri Myrddin. There are also numerous art and craft galleries, potteries and studios throughout the Tywi valley, especially in the towns of Llandeilo, Carmarthen and Llandovery.

Such a thriving arts community is a great asset to the Tywi valley, and the many village and town halls are constantly in use for every kind of cultural and artistic event. Owing to their relatively unspoilt character, the town and village landscapes are much in demand with film-makers as locations for movies; indeed the whole valley, with so many different views and backdrops within a comparatively small area, has proved ideal for both documentary and feature films.

All in all, the cultural life of the valley, like the river itself, combines the contemporary, historic and timeless in a most inspirational way.

ELERI RETALLICK

Llanegwad Church morning mist.

Japanese Garden.

Paxton's Tower.

Maypole at the National Botanic Gardens.

No. 18   From Folly to Wonder

It was a chance conversation in a nearby pub that took us to Paxton's Tower.

There were as many stories about how this folly came to be as there were drinkers in the pub, it seemed. New to Carmarthenshire as we were, we assumed what we were being told was part myth, part mischief-making. But we knew we had to take a closer look.

It was a warm, still, almost balmy, late-September afternoon with barely a breath of wind or a cloud in the sky. We gazed in awe from beside the tower at the landscape laid out before us. And what a landscape! The silver streak of river snaking its way unhurriedly down the valley, looping lazily left and right in the lea of *Lord of the Rings*-like castle ruins. Wonderful!

The real wonder of it – to the two of us, at least, standing right there, right then – was that we were alone. Could this sparklingly special sight be a secret to all but us? It seemed unfathomable. Why was the car park not crowded with cars? Why was the hillside not packed with picnickers making the most of the last of the summery sun and this most glorious of vistas?

And speaking of wonders . . .

The short walk downhill back to the car park reveals another: the recently-crowned No. 1 Modern Wonder of Wales, the Norman-Foster-designed Great Glasshouse; the joyous, iconic centrepiece of the National Botanic Garden of Wales. It has been described – much more eloquently – thus: 'this giant dome of glass reflects the gentle contours and muted colours of the surrounding Welsh hills. In certain light, it glitters like an immense raindrop, resting deep in the Tywi Valley.'

This amazing sight – 'a cathedral of geometry and light' – does not diminish, not even the thousandth time you see it. And the more you find out about the largest single-span glasshouse in the world, the more of a wonder it becomes; for instance, did you know each one of the 785 panes of glass that go to make up the 4,500 metres of dome weighs a tonne and that every single one is unique?

The Garden has much more to offer, of course, in its sumptuous 600 acres. It can transport you to extremes: from the sheer exuberance of the schools' 'veg plot' project to the quiet contemplation of the Japanese Garden; from mirror pool to mini farm; from the physicans' garden to the forgotten falls.

Like any 'wonder', though, it really has to be seen to be believed.

DAVID HARDY

Low cloud over the river from Merlin's Hill.

Carmarthen Castle gatehouse.

No. 19   My Bishop's Palace

Until recently, it seems to me that the beauty of the Tywi valley was a well-kept secret. However, I have known about this special place for many years, as my place of work is Carmarthenshire County Museum, at Abergwili, in the heart of the valley.

Why is Abergwili special? For a start, working here makes it impossible to be unaware of the changing seasons and the presence of the river Tywi, an immense force of nature. Everyday brings something new to see on the journey to work. Sometimes it is the shimmering silver light of floodwater covering almost the entire valley. At other times, low-lying, early morning mist clings to the valley bottom obscuring everything except the spire of Abergwili church. In high summer, cattle wade into the Gwili or drink from the Tywi itself, at one of the bends in the river. The building of Carmarthen's eastern bypass has given even greater opportunities to enjoy the valley and provided a spectacular new view of the town itself that reminds me of an 18th-century engraving.

Abergwili's long history also makes it special. What could be better than a county museum in an ancient building in a beautiful setting? In medieval times the building was a college and later became the Palace of the Bishops of St David's. The museum is surrounded by gardens and the remnants of a landscaped park, designed to present views of the river. Unfortunately, the river decided to veer away from the palace in 1802, when it cut a new course after a flood, so that a small canal had to be built to connect the palace to the river. Looming above the museum is one of the Tywi valley's characteristic hills, Merlin's Hill. This too is an ancient site and has the remains of an Iron Age hill fort. Merlin's Hill is also a place of legend, as it is said to have been the home of Merlin the Magician for a while.

It is for all of these reasons that I find the museum and its setting marvellous. There is a kind of perfection in the marriage between Carmarthenshire County Museum, its historic building and its setting in the Tywi valley.

ANN DORSETT

Market and clocktower, Carmarthen.

Carmarthen quay and bridge.

New and old bridges, quayside, Carmarthen.

No. 20   Walks on the Wild Side

Slow travel, like slow food, allows time for deep appreciation and enjoyment. Not only does walking a landscape connect one to it as no other form of travel can; but walkers can reach parts of the valley inaccessible by road. Although the A40 between Llandovery and Carmarthen gently immerses the traveller in the landscape of the mid-Tywi valley, it misses out the upper and lower reaches of the river, its flood plain, and the hills with magnificent distant views, which border it on each side.

From the source of the river in the remote wilderness beyond the Tywi Forest in mid-Wales; down to the sea at Llansteffan and Ferryside where there are stunning panoramic views of the estuary widening into Carmarthen Bay from Llansteffan Castle and Tregoning Hill, the finest views reward those who explore on foot.

Experience the joys of encountering the natural world at close quarters: a pair of foxes emerging from tussocks near the source of the Tywi; the drama of water crashing over rocks where the Doethie meets the youthful Tywi alongside the RSPB Dinas reserve; woods carpeted with bluebells or the gold of kingcups; ancient woodland running down to the river; historic parkland with magnificent specimen trees; traditional Welsh Black and White Park cattle, fields of sheep and lambs, and the dairy herds for which Carmarthenshire is renowned. Marvel at the miniature beauty of lichens thriving in clean air; birds, insects and butterflies in the meadows and hedgerows, a heron rising from the river; a swan nesting on the Bishop's Pond at Abergwili; the green filigree of ferns in woods and hedgerows; the sun setting over the valley from the panoramic viewpoint of a castle. Breathe in the scents of flower-spangled hedge-banks; sense from the old houses and traditional farm buildings how life was lived in the rural Tywi valley, then see the displays of rural life at the museum at Abergwili. Discover a pool to swim in, ancient green lanes, gateposts made from stone slabs or whole tree trunks in the round, a wealth of fungi in spring and autumn. And experience them all from a series of dramatic vantage points.

PAULINE SYKES

A walk through Castle Woods, Llandeilo.

Carmarthen to Llansteffan

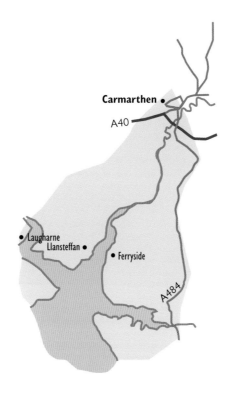

Carmarthen from Castle Woods.

No. 21

If You Go Down to the Woods . . .

Green Castle Woods straddle the road from Carmarthen to Llansteffan, near Llangain.

Now managed by the Woodland Trust they are made up of three woods with open areas that cover 125 acres. They contain a unique variety of habitats. Apart from the ancient woodland there are fields used for grazing cattle, several acres of newly planted woodland, flowering meadow, partly coppiced wet woodland, ancient hedgerows (known to date from 1779), two quarries, and streams that provide a restful sound in the deep, quiet woodland. At two points the paths provide striking views of the Tywi valley and surrounding countryside. The castle referred to was a fortified mansion, probably dating from 1500. Its ruins stand in the garden of the farmhouse, which was built out of the gatehouse.

The southern boundary of the wood is the River Tywi, where there used to be a quay, where wine came in from France and building stone and farm produce were shipped up to Carmarthen.

Two of the ancient woodlands are largely oak; the third and wetter wood contains ash, oak, birch, alder and willow. This land is abundant in fallen wood, which in turn encourages fungi and beetles.

In May large areas of bluebells are a breathtaking sight, whilst in the damper areas these are followed by wild garlic with its characteristic smell. Later in the summer, when the leaf canopy

Entrance to Green Castle Woods.

provides deep shade with patchy sunlight, there are dog roses; the autumn then brings the red berries in the rowan trees, blackberries and sloes. Badgers are the largest animals in the woods, but birds and insects abound. Owl nesting boxes have been placed in the trees and most have been used. There is even a seat for carved owls!

A complete network of paths has been opened by a small group of volunteer 'Woodlanders', who maintain them throughout the year. Here, there are rich findings for botanists and biologists, but also great pleasure for dog walkers, ramblers, dreamers, and all who enjoy the variety and magic of ancient woodland.

KEITH GREENLAW

Estuary view from Llansteffan Castle.

The footpath along the estuary.

Cockle-pickers on the sands.

I Say 'Tywi', You Say 'Towy'

River names are aboriginal. Rivers were baptised, so to speak, by the earliest people to make their acquaintance. And the names they gave them seldom changed. Events and ownership have altered dry-land names but not rivers. Over time, dialect will colour pronunciation so that name and meaning often become corrupted and lost. Such has happened to Tywi. No one knows for certain what it means, but we can guess intelligently.

It is reasonable to suppose that the rivers of Great Britain were given names any time after the last Ice Age receded, some ten thousand years ago. River names familiar to us were, in some form, familiar also as the daily parlance of the people who built megaliths at Pentre Ifan and Stonehenge. What has come down to us are 'filtered' versions of those original names, already time-worn when spoken by Bronze Age farmers and later iron-equipped Celts who, in the last millennium BC, spoke in Brythonic and Goidelic dialects of an earlier, Indo-European-derived language.

It was in the decade that begins in 140 AD that the name 'Tywi' first made its appearance in a written form that survived. The Romans had been present in Wales for a hundred and eighty years when the Greek geographer Ptolemy records the name in his guide to geography, *Geographike hypegensis*. He leaves us with a pretty accurate idea of the sound of the name as spoken, when he records 'Tywi' as *Touʃ'os* (pronounced Touiios). In Latin it was written '*Tobius*' (pronounced *Towi-us)*. Classical nouns necessarily appended a gender suffix '*os*' (in Greek) or '*us*' (in Latin). From this, we can safely assume that Ptolemy's source-reference would have been heard as something closely resembling '*Towie*', as the Brythonic noun had a weak '*i*' gender-ending.

The earliest Welsh orthography – in the eleven hundreds – usually rendered this as '*Tywi*', and this continues pretty consistently though from the 12th to the 17th centuries with variants such as '*Tewi*' or '*Tewy*'. The form '*Towy*' is also recorded in Welsh between the 12th and the 16th centuries. No significance should be read into these differing versions. Before standardised spelling, writers wrote to the sound of their own voices, recording on paper what they heard. Spelling would reflect the speaker's social status as well as regional accent. Often, writers simply followed a written precedent. Leland, writing between 1536 and 1539, renders the name '*Tewi*'. Camden, Drayton and Edward Lhuyd writing in the 17th century, as classically-educated scholars, can be seen to have relied on Ptolemy rather than their ears – opting for the 'o'-sound, rather than the Welsh '*ew*' sound after the initial 'T': the one thing all seem to be agreed upon!

Among the principal scholars who have made the origin and meaning of Welsh place names, and the names of rivers in particular, their special study during the last century are R.J. Thomas in his *Enwau Afonydd a Nentydd Cymru* (Names of Welsh Rivers and Brooks), 1938, and Professor Kenneth Jackson in *Language and History in Early Britain*, both works of the highest scholarship. Between them, they are not, unfortunately, able to throw very much light on the origin of the name Tywi, except to conclude that its derivation is older than any known language.

R.J. Thomas suggests that the name, in common with river names based on the root 'Tam', possibly means 'to swell or grow' – as contained within the Latin-derived word 'tumescent'.

The origin of this name (Tywi) is very obscure. The consolidation of the root '*tewa-*', '*tou* ', '*te* ' becomes apparent, as seen in the Welsh '*tyfu*' ('to grow'), the Irish '*teo*' ('strength'), the Latin '*tumeo*' ('to swell'), the Sanskrit '*tavas*' ('powerful'): cf. R Taw, Devon. 'Strong river' is the right description for this type of river.

Also, incidentally, the root '*tyw-*' in the (Welsh) word '*tywyll*' ('dark') is apparent, though it does not shed any great light on the name under scrutiny as, from what I have seen of them, Tywi's waters are dark, as Lewys Glyn Cothi (15th century) says:

> *Nid av vi i Dywi, val dall*
> *Neu ddwr gwineuddu arall.*
> ('I will not go to Towy as a blind man
> Nor to any other wine-dark water.')

Thomas notes the '*Gwineu*' connection – as a primal Tywi tributary – but apparently misses Glyn Cothi's allusion to the Gwinau, 'fused' to Llyn Du in the same image and breath: '*gwineuddu*'.

Jackson agrees with Thomas's '*Tam*'-root interpretation, which embraces *Taw, Tawe, Tamar* and even *Thames*. Considered alongside the Welsh word '*tyfu*', '*Teifi*' is a clearer example of the concept. Jackson examines the possibility of Du – from Llyn Du (Dark or Black Lake), situated half a mile or so above the source of the Tywi – leading to '*Dewi*', as a root of derivation, but without any great conviction.

Scientifically, it would be possible today to prove – or otherwise – hydrographic connection between Llyn Du and the Tywi system. It is less than likely that the descendants of Neolithic man would have made that association.

When Julius Caesar first came ashore in Britain he marvelled, in his *Gallic Wars*, at the twice-daily ebb and flow of the tides, something he had never seen before. Similarly, people only accustomed to constant-flow, ground-fed or artesian-well-sprung rivers, such as those that run off Salisbury Plain, would have found engrossment of a river during a flood or tidal event remarkable enough to single out this characteristic and label it – as a precaution to themselves and to others – along the lines of 'Sweller', 'Grower' or 'Fattener'. In both Jones and Jackson there is affirmation that this characteristic, observed long ago, is a name-source of specific British spate-rivers.

Modern Welsh '*Tywi*', spoken in native 'Carmarthenshire', produces precisely the same open-vowelled sound as its English version, 'Towy': though a non-Welsh-speaking reader would easily not realise this. 'River Towy' is the logical English-language rendering of '*Afon Tywi*' – as 'River Wye' is English for '*Afon Gwy*', and '*Afon Wysg*' Welsh for 'River Usk'. A generation has recently grown up which is heard to refer in English conversation to the 'Teewee', as this is how it must appear to an English eye. Sadly, this convention is the product of wrong-headed political manipulation, based in ignorance.

LYNN HUGHES

The Timeless Tywi.

Train entering Ferryside.

Llansteffan Castle.

Llansteffan Castle from Ferryside.

As the River Tywi flows south-westwards, from its source in the Cambrian Mountains to its mouth in Carmarthen Bay, it passes through a landscape steeped in Welsh history. The story of human activity in the valley dates from the hunter-gatherers of the Ice Age, through the earliest farming communities of the Neolithic to the monument builders of the Bronze and Iron Ages. During the first century AD, the valley resounded to the noise of Roman hobnail boots marching along the new military road between the garrison forts at Llandovery, Llandeilo and Carmarthen. The Roman occupation saw the establishment of the civilian settlement at Carmarthen, Wales's oldest town, while the end of Roman rule heralded an age of princes and saints who made their own important cultural mark on the valley landscape. Later still, the violent turmoil of the years between 1100 and 1300, saw Anglo-Norman lords and Welsh princes fight for political control of the valley. This period has left an extraordinary concentration of medieval castles; a group that rivals those in any other area of Europe, both in terms of their numbers and their dramatic settings. Between the late 17th century and the mid-19th century, the valley provided the setting for a unique group of planned parks and gardens as the artists and architects of the Picturesque movement recognised the wonderful backdrop that the great beauty of the valley could provide. The widespread popular sense of the Tywi valley as a cherished landscape extends into the present day. The gardens and the castles, the hills and the river, provide a magnet for visitors who seek that unique blend of history and nature that the Tywi Valley can provide.

Prehistoric settlement and burial sites (c4000BC – cAD70)

The first farmers. It is possible that the story of human activity in the Tywi valley dates back tens of thousands of years when hunter gatherers ventured into the area during the warmer phases of the Ice Age. However, the first farmers did not settle in the valley until about 4000 BC, probably growing wheat and barley and bringing with them herds of cattle, sheep and goats. The evidence for their

early settlements is elusive. Indeed they may have continued to lead a semi-nomadic existence moving around the landscape and only settling in any one place for a short period of time. Evidence for their presence in the Tywi valley is provided by occasional finds of stone axes, used to clear the woodland for farming, and several 'public' ritual monuments. The chambered tomb at Gelli near Rhandir-mwyn in the upper Tywi valley is typical of dozens of small stone monuments built to house human remains that are scattered throughout Pembrokeshire and Carmarthenshire. A more unusual monument is the group of standing stones associated with an oval bank and ditch at Ffynnon Newydd, Nantgaredig. Such monuments are possibly associated with a deep spiritual link with the ancestors.

The earliest metal workers. By 2000 BC new styles of pottery and a new technology, bronze working, appear in west Wales. Although the evidence for the settlements and fields of these Bronze Age folk remain rare, the area of the Tywi is dotted by burial mounds and standing stones that demonstrate that they had a very real presence in the valley. The large cairns on the hill and mountain summits flanking the valley suggest that many of these monuments were meant to be seen over a wide area. Spectacular examples can be seen at Tair Carn Uchaf and Tair Carn Isaf on the ridge overlooking Carreg Cennen Castle. The earthen mounds or stone cairns generally covered deposits of cremated bone and pottery urns. By contrast many of the standing stones are located on the valley floor and a good example can be seen at Abermarlais near Llangadog. These enigmatic monuments appear to have acted as physical and spiritual markers in the landscape although their precise purpose is far from clear.

The Iron Age. The adoption of iron working after 800 BC also sees the first clear evidence for settled communities in Carmarthenshire. These are largely scattered farmsteads, usually surrounded by an earthwork bank and ditch. They are generally small and they are unlikely to have housed more than an extended family. However, amongst these farms are much larger fortified sites of apparently higher status. These hill forts, such as Merlin's Hill, are located on prominent hills overlooking the valley. The greatest of all is the massive hill fort at Garn Goch that towers over the central Tywi valley at Bethlehem near Llandeilo. This is one of the largest hill forts in Wales. It seems possible that the hill forts were the seats of local chiefs and may have been used as places of refuge for the surrounding population in times of trouble.

The Roman occupation (cAD70 – AD410)

The conquest. Although the Romans arrived in Britain in AD 43, the conquest of Wales was not complete until several decades later. At the time of the conquest the Tywi valley, and the rest of south-west Wales, was occupied by an Iron Age tribal grouping known as the Demetae. It has been argued that the Demetae put up a relatively light resistance to Roman rule. However, the presence of substantial Roman military garrisons at Llandovery, Llandeilo, Pumsaint and Carmarthen suggests that they were no walk-over. During the conquest period, large marching camps, occupied by the legions while on campaign, were established at Y Pigwn and Arosfa Garreg Lwyd. The traces of the earthworks surrounding these camps can still be seen in the Upper Usk valley above Llandovery. The more permanent garrison forts were built to police the newly conquered territory. The fort at Llandovery (Alabum) later became the site of the church of Llanfair-ar-y-bryn while the fort at Carmarthen (Maridunum) now lies beneath Spilman Street, near to the town centre. On the River Cothi, the fort at Pumsaint overlooked the Roman gold-mines of Dolaucothi. The site of two superimposed forts of different dates at Llandeilo came to light in spectacular fashion during a geophysical survey in the eastern part of Dinefwr Park in 2003. The earlier of the two forts is one of the largest in Wales.

Roads and towns. During the early second century AD the forts were abandoned and the Tywi valley settled down to the Roman way of life for the next 300 years. The military road, built to link the former garrisons of the valley, was now converted to civilian use. The line of this road became one of the great route corridors through South Wales. It became known as the 'High Road' and the modern A40 still follows approximately the same route. Immediately following the conquest, small civilian settlements had grown up alongside this road outside the entrances to each of the forts. At Carmarthen, this settlement grew into the *civitas* capital of the Demetae; one of only two major towns in Roman Wales. The town defences were refortified in stone in the third century AD and an amphitheatre was built just outside the east gate. Incredibly, the plan of the Roman town can still be traced in the modern street plan of Carmarthen. Present streets follow the line of the defences and the modern Priory Street approximately follows the line of the main east-west Roman Street. St Peter's church appears to have been built over the Roman town's west gate.

The Middle Ages (AD 410 – AD1560)

The age of the Saints. By the early fifth century Roman rule had come to an end. However, the Celtic rulers who followed claimed Roman ancestry and authority and retained their Christian faith, which had been introduced into Wales during the late Roman period. During the fifth and sixth centuries Christian evangelists established churches and religious settlements throughout the valley and many of them, including St Teilo, St Cadog, St Dyfan and St Tybie, are commemorated in the many 'Llan' place names. Early Christian stones with decorated incised crosses are a feature of the west Wales landscape. An important early text was a unique illustrated gospel book that was, for two hundred years, located in the church of St Teilo in Llandeilo, before it was acquired by Lichfield Cathedral in the eleventh century. The cultural significance of this book is enhanced by the presence of marginal notes in the earliest surviving written Welsh dating to the ninth and tenth centuries. A digital copy of the gospels is now on display in the church along with two fine early Christian stone crosses.

The age of the castle. By the ninth century the small kingdom of Ystrad Tywi became part of Deheubarth ruled by Hywel Dda who is credited with drawing up a Welsh law code. However, the two hundred years between 1100 and 1300 were turbulent ones for the Tywi valley as the Welsh princes and Anglo-Norman lords wrestled for control of the area. This is reflected in the dense concentration of both Anglo-Norman and Welsh castles, which together comprise some of Britain's finest medieval sites. The important masonry castles at Kidwelly, Laugharne and Llansteffan in the Tywi and Taf estuaries were established by Norman lords, while Henry I established a royal castle at Carmarthen. Meanwhile, in the north east, a separate Norman incursion resulted in the establishment of motte and bailey castles at Llandovery and Castell Meurig near Llangadog. However, the heart of the valley, Cantref Mawr and Cwmwd Iscennen, remained in Welsh hands until the later 13th century and the Welsh princes established the castles of Dryslwyn, Dinefwr and Carreg Cennen. The best known of these princes was Rhys ap Gruffudd, the Lord Rhys, who established his capital at Dinefwr in the mid-12th century.

Medieval towns and villages. An essential part of the Anglo-Norman conquest was the creation of towns, such as Llansteffan, Carmarthen and Llandovery, in the shadow of the newly constructed castles. At Carmarthen the new Anglo-Norman town existed alongside the old Welsh settlement that had developed on the site of the former Roman town. Perhaps in imitation of the new Anglo-Norman boroughs, the Welsh princes also established towns adjacent to their castles at Dryslwn and Dinefwr. Following the capture of Dinefwr in the later 13th century, a new English borough was established at Newton, several hundred metres away. However, neither settlement was able to compete with the growing influence of the former religious settlement at nearby Llandeilo.

The English political conquest of the valley was complete by the end of the 13th century, and new settlers were to establish a significant presence in the new towns. However, they were to be dramatically shaken by the Glyndŵr rebellion of the early 15th century. This uprising was to generate its own local Welsh folk heroes, such as Llywelyn ap Gruffudd Fychan, who is now commemorated by a statue at Llandovery.

Elsewhere, there were few nucleated villages dating from the medieval period. Some grew around medieval churches in the late 13th century under the influence of the bishops, such as at Abergwili, Llanegwad and the borough of Llangadog. However, many medieval churches in the valley, which still form distinctive landmarks of the countryside, had little influence on medieval settlement. Others were to become the focal points for later communities such as Llanarthne and Cil-y-cwm.

The post-medieval period (AD1560 – Present)

Transport and industry. The Tywi valley sits just outside the South Wales coalfield and so has not seen the levels of industrialisation experienced to the south and east. Despite an early tinplate works, established in 1748, Carmarthen is not characterised by its industrial heritage. Many of the industries of the valley were linked to the agricultural economy such as woollen mills, tanneries and sawmills. However, above the valley, on the Black Mountain, are found the pits, kilns and spoil heaps of the 18th and 19th-century limestone quarrying industry. The Tywi valley has provided one of the great route corridors through South Wales since Roman times. The 'High Road' (the A40) was supplemented by the railway line from Carmarthen to Llandovery in 1858 and several of the stations, such as Nantgaredig, became the focal points for new settlements. The Heart of Wales line still runs through part of the Tywi valley and onto the great viaduct at Cynghordy.

The country estates. The landscaped parks and gardens, created by the great gentry estates of the 17th, 18th and early 19th centuries, provide perhaps the most outstanding historical legacy of the valley. The great estates and parks include those of the Vaughans at Gelli Aur, the Rices at Dinefwr, the Dyers at Aberglasney, the Joneses at Abermarlais and the Paxtons and Abadam families at Middleton Hall. The latter has now become the site of the National Botanical Garden of Wales. Not all of the great houses themselves have survived. However, all the estates retain elements of their historic buildings, walled and terraced gardens and planted trees and groves. As a group they are of truly international importance and their historic and artistic resonances have created the popular sense of a cherished landscape enjoyed by visitor and resident alike. The Tywi valley truly is, as Mererid Hopwood reminds us in her foreword, the 'Garden of Wales'.

GWILYM HUGHES

Notes on photographs and locations

* References are to   OS Landranger 1:50,000 Sheets 146, 147, 159, 160.
                             OS Explorer 1:25,000 Sheets 177, 186, 187, Outdoor Leisure 12.

Notes on Photography

It is almost a cliché, but it is still worth saying that it's not the equipment that takes the picture; it's the eye. My own experience is that, certainly with the best shots, the picture is taken with the mind's eye before the camera is even picked up. The equipment should capture as nearly as possible what is in the mind's eye, and in doing so, get in the way as little as possible. Having said that, the camera, lenses and recording medium should be capable of delivering the desired result. There are a number of camera and lens makers producing excellent equipment, and any one of them is capable of making high quality images.

I rarely use a tripod, partly because I resent the encumbrance, but mainly because with most equipment and in most situations it is not necessary. Low light and long focal length lens make one useful. There are two images of mine in the book where a tripod was essential, both where a 300mm lens was used, and several others where parapets of bridges, car doors and other convenient fixed points were used as rests.

During the final stages of taking pictures, I made the change from film to digital. It was a reluctant change, but an expedient one. About 10% of the images in the book are digitally captured.

Equipment used by me:
Film Capture
Olympus OM4ti camera body
Olympus OM2n camera body
Olympus Zuiko 28mm f2.8 lens
Olympus Zuiko 50mm f1.8 lens
Olympus Zuiko 90mm f2 lens
Tamron SP 180mm f2.5 lens
Olympus Zuiko 300mm f4.5 lens
Film type: Fujichrome Velvia 50 ISO
Digital Capture
Fujifilm S2 Pro camera body
Sigma EX 17 –35mm f2.8 AF lens
Nikon 50mm f1.8 AF lens
Nikon 35 – 105mm f3.5 – 4.5 AF lens
ISO setting: 100
Shooting format: RAW

Equipment used by Graham Rankin:
Leica R8 camera body
100mm APO Macro Elmart-R
35-70mm Vario Elmar-R
Film type: Fujichrome Velvia 50 ISO

Notes on Contributors

David Rees was, at the time of writing, a conservation manager with the Forestry Commission.

Isabel Macho is a conservation officer with Carmarthenshire County Council.

Martin Humphreys is an RSPB warden for the Dinas/Gwenffrwd and Cwm Clydach reserves. He lives in Swansea.

Rhobert ap Steffan is an author, historian and photographer who lives in Llangadog.

Owain Gruffydd lives in Ffairfach and works in Llandeilo as Director of Menter Bro Dinefwr

Rev. Mike Cottam is vicar of St Cadog's in Llangadog, having previously been a farmer in Pembrokeshire and a cowboy in Canada.

Gwilym Hughes lives in Llandeilo and is Director of Cambria Archaeology.

Jason Lawday is Footpaths Ranger in the Tywi valley and lives in Bethlehem.

Phillip James is a senior manager with the National Trust in South Wales, and lives in Cwmdu.

Pam Steane Price is an archaeologist, organic farmer and grower of herbs. She has lifelong interests in environmental issues and local history.

Lynn Hughes is an historian, author of numerous books and passionate fisherman. He lives in Gelli Aur.

Graham Rankin is Director of Operations at Aberglasne Gardens and specialises in plant photography.

Ian Morgan is a consultant ecologist who was formerly a senior scientist with Countryside Council for Wales.

Eleri Retallick is Principal Arts Officer with Carmarthenshire County Council and was formerly Director of the Miners' Theatre in Ammanford.

David Hardy is a media consultant and former editor of *The Carmarthen Journal*.

Pauline Sykes is passionate about walking and environmental issues. She has her own website about walking called www.walkcarmarthenshire.com.

Keith Greenlaw is a volunteer Woodlander with the Woodland Trust.

Ann Dorsett is a curator at the Carmarthenshire County Museum in Abergwili.

Acknowledgements

Firstly, I have to thank all the contributors to this book, whose local knowledge and passion made this book something powerfully different from a collection of pretty pictures. David Fielding, as editor of *Carmarthenshire Life*, gave me my first break into local publishing by featuring many of my photographs on the front cover and elsewhere in his beautiful magazine. His continuing support extended to encouraging my writing skills and including a number of my articles in recent years. Graham Rankin, Director of Aberglasney Gardens, was one of the few who saw the need for *Beloved Tywi*, and whose skill with a camera is such that I am delighted to include his images of the gardens as the only photographs not taken by me. Alan Enoch, Conservation Ranger with the Forestry Commission, patiently guided me on my quest for the source of the Tywi. Dai Williams, Mynachdy, gave me encouragement in the early days of my mad ideas and whose bilingual erudition so easily sorted out seemingly tricky translations. Gwilym Hughes, Director of Cambria Archaeology, enthusiastically embraced the idea and wrote the fascinating history of Tywi. Dr David Jones was kind enough to organise and star in the fisherman-in-the-river photograph. Ceri Wyn Jones and the team at Gomer not only liked the notion of the first ever photographic study of the Tywi, but also gently pushed and pulled me and put together this amazing thing. Finally, and most importantly, my family who saw it through with me, encouraging, supporting and commenting throughout the long journey.